IT AIN'T ABOUT THE MONEY

IT AIN'T ABOUT THE MONEY

A Coach's Quest for Purpose, Impact, and Creating a Life that Matters

Greg Logsdon

Published by Game Changer Publishing

Paperback ISBN: 978-1-969372-14-8

Hardcover ISBN: 978-1-969372-15-5

Digital ISBN: 978-1-969372-16-2

www.GameChangerPublishing.com

I want to thank my wife, Rachel, and my daughters, Conner and Addie. I wake up and go to sleep every day thinking about them, and my love for them is over the moon.

A special thanks to my mom—for her patience, her strength, and all she did to raise me. Everything I know about how to treat people well, I learned by watching her. Raised in a single-parent home in rural Missouri, I had a front-row seat to my mom's daily acts of generosity and grit. I'm forever grateful.

When you're related to, married to, or live with a coach, you make many sacrifices, and my mom and family have made more than their share. Thank you guys, I love you.

THANK YOU FOR PURCHASING AND READING MY BOOK

Let's connect!

Scan the QR Code:

IT AIN'T ABOUT THE MONEY

A Coach's Quest for Purpose, Impact,
and Creating a Life that Matters

GREG LOGSDON

FOREWORD

Walking into Rock Bridge High School in Columbia, MO, in the summer of 2020, I had no idea what to expect. Making the drive from Kansas City, my 14-year-old daughter, Abigail, and I arrived almost two hours early for her first team practice with the Missouri Phenom Nike youth basketball team.

Abigail had received an invite from Phenom's founder, Reggie Middlebrook, and we had heard nothing but great things about the program. The reality was, though, we didn't know anyone involved, including the person who would actually coach her team. Of course, when you arrive early at a public high school on a Saturday morning, the gym doors are locked and the parking lot is empty.

We stood outside for only a few minutes before out comes this Greg Logsdon guy, who had already been inside preparing for all the Phenom practices that day. He let us into the gym, and the first thing Greg did (despite his many other responsibilities) was rebound for Abigail as she warmed up early for her team's practice. We immediately felt welcome, and I watched how Greg quickly built a relationship with Abigail.

Greg's energy was contagious. His big stature was only exceeded by his engaging personality. Little did Abigail and I know, this was the start of a friendship that would have as much impact on me as it did on her.

The next year, Greg became Abigail's EYBL head coach. He not only led her team as they competed for a summer championship in the toughest youth league in the country, Nike EYBL, but he also became our close friend and confidant. Coaching for all the right reasons, Greg is a natural-born leader with a big heart and a passion for making an impact on players on and off the court. He is honest, always his authentic self, and somehow finds endless quality time to offer advice to aspiring players and interested parents.

Reading everything I just shared, you probably think Greg only coaches as his profession. I mean, how else can someone be so successful in a particular occupation and have such wide-ranging admiration and impact? Well, Greg isn't just a revered coach. He has had the Midas touch in many other parts of his life too. Among a broad collection of businesses, Greg has built a real estate portfolio spanning hotels, residential properties, and student housing. His entrepreneurial spirit and leadership abilities run so deep that Greg is regarded as the leading medical device partner for spine and neck surgeons in the bi-state region of Missouri and Kansas.

Finally, saving the best for last, Greg is a dedicated father of two girls and a devout husband to Rachel.

By way of introduction, my whole life has somehow been underpinned by sports, whether as a participant, a player, a fan, or, more recently, as an owner of one of the most highly valued and successful women's professional sports teams in the world (according to *Forbes*). As the majority co-owner of two soccer teams, the Kansas City Current and HB Koge Women, a top-division Denmark team, as well as a former Division I basketball player at Princeton University, I know firsthand how special it is to learn from the "Greg Logsdons" in sports. These are the selfless leaders who truly found a calling to coach. Greg answered the call, cares deeply about his impact, and has delivered for countless student-athletes over his career. His ability to understand the technical aspects of the game while never losing sight of player relationships and player development has enriched many young lives.

Greg's book is a must-read. It is full of storytelling and is designed to be helpful to a wide variety of people who not only coach but lead. Greg brings forth so many lessons learned over decades of coaching, including some that are rarely touched upon: navigating challenges (including difficult parents), balancing life while coaching, and, finally, a true introspection on why we coach. It is inspirational, instructive, and a book that truly should be part of a continuing required education course for coaches interested in lifelong lessons from a coaching legend.

Chris Long
Founder and Co-Owner, Kansas City Current
Co-Owner, HB Koge Women
Founder and Chief Executive Officer, Palmer Square
Capital Management LLC
Founder and Chief Executive Officer, Palmer Square Real
Estate Management LLC

CONTENTS

INTRODUCTION

I've always wanted to write a book. It's been one of those bucket-list items I kept tucked in the back of my mind for years. So when the opportunity came—thanks to modern technology and a little friendly pressure from some longtime friends and colleagues—I finally decided to go for it.

I grew up a storyteller in a small town in rural Northeast Missouri. Storytelling was what we did. We'd gather around the dinner table, the fireplace, or the living room and tell stories— some true, some *maybe* not so true. My grandpa Ed was the ulti-mate storyteller. He was the detail guy, spinning tales that could make you laugh, cry, or scratch your head. So to write a book in that same storytelling spirit feels like coming full circle.

Part of my intent with this book is to share a few laughs with families, ease some of the pressure coaches often feel, and offer valuable tips for young, aspiring coaches on how to get started and balance normal everyday life. Coaching, after all, is full of stories—whether you're talking to your team, swapping tales with fellow coaches, or sharing lessons with your players. Hopefully, this book gives you a few stories worth retelling, along with practical advice and encouragement along the way.

WHY DID I WRITE THIS BOOK?

I started coaching in 1991. My first job—more on that later—was coaching track and field, a sport I loved in both high school and college. Even though it involved a lot of running (which, let's be honest, isn't always fun), it brought me great joy. Now, with over thirty years of coaching experience, I've collected a wealth of lessons, stories, and meaningful long-term relationships with colleagues, players, and families. This book is my chance to share some of those stories and reflect on what I've learned along the way. It's written for coaches of all levels—whether you're just starting out or you've been at it for decades. Coaching today comes with challenges that didn't exist twenty or thirty years ago: more stress, tighter schedules, and increased pressure from parents and communities. My hope is to give back by helping coaches find their way in balancing coaching, family, and a fulfilling personal life.

WHO IS THIS BOOK FOR?

It's for new coaches trying to find their footing. It's for seasoned coaches who might be looking for a fresh perspective. And it's for anyone who's ever thought, *I'd love to coach, but I don't know how I'd make it all work.*

If that's you, I want to offer encouragement and some tangible next steps. Coaching has brought me deep fulfillment—so much more than just wins and losses—and I hope you'll walk away from this book with ideas and inspiration to pursue the same.

So, am I an expert? No. Do I still learn something new every day from coaching? Absolutely. After three decades in the game, if even a few stories or tips in this book help you along your journey, then it will have served its purpose.

WHAT CAN YOU EXPECT?

Plenty of laughs and smiles, I hope. A few eye rolls, maybe. But mostly, real-life stories that reflect the highs and lows of coaching. You'll find practical insights, encouragement, and hopefully a little inspiration to keep showing up—for your players, your team, and yourself. And if you're someone who's been on the sidelines—wanting to coach but unsure how to make it work with your family, job, or lifestyle—I hope this book inspires you to take that step.

Finally, I want every reader to understand this: if you coach a team at any level, the impact you have on the lives of others is significant. Coaching gives you a chance to make a lasting impact. Never underestimate the influence you have and the difference you can make. It's never about the trophies or titles, but always about the people.

So with that, let's jump in.

PART ONE
ROSTER BUILDING
THE PEOPLE WHO SHAPE US, THE LESSONS THAT BUILD US

CHAPTER 1
DO PEOPLE REALLY EAT CHICKEN WINGS?

D o people really eat chicken wings?

Well, I know Thaddeus Hamilton eats 'em, along with movie theater popcorn. He could survive on those two meals alone!

But what does that have to do with coaching?

My high school football and track coach—who also happened to be an assistant basketball coach at the local college—was going to scout a college game in Fayette one night. It was the middle of winter, one of those cold, snowy Missouri days. I swear it snowed more back then, or at least it felt that way growing up in northeast Missouri. He needed someone to ride with him, so he gave me a call.

The rotary phone rang at the house (we didn't have cellphones back then), and I picked it up. It was Coach Hamilton. He grew up in Atlanta, neighbors with Martin Luther King Jr., and had gone on to play running back at Culver-Stockton College in Canton, Missouri. Now teaching geometry and coaching at Highland High

School, he wasn't only a great coach, but he was the kind of role model who connected with his players and looked out for them.

"Hey," he said, "I've got to drive to Fayette tonight. Want to go scout the game with me? I'll come pick you up and grab us some dinner."

He knew I was a big basketball guy, and I quickly agreed. I was in ninth grade at the time and still remember the car he drove, a red two-door Mazda 323. I was already about 6'5", and he was a big guy too, so we were quite a sight—squeezed into that little car, heading off to scout a college game.

I jumped in the car, and he handed me a bag of food. I figured we'd both eat on the road, him behind the wheel and me in the passenger seat. He opens his, and I glance over. *Man*, I thought, *that looks terrible. People don't really eat that, do they?*

I asked him, "What did you get me?" and opened mine up.

He smiled and said, "I got you the same thing. I thought you'd like it. JK's in Canton has the best chicken wings around!"

Sure enough, it was chicken wings.

I looked at him, kind of confused. "Coach Hamilton, do people actually eat chicken wings?"

See, I grew up on a farm. We ate chicken breasts, legs, and thighs. Wings? We threw those out to the pigs, sheep, goats, and whatever wild animals were roaming the pasture. We thought wings were the bottom of the barrel. But that little moment, of a coach going out of his way and providing me a meal, has stuck with me for decades.

As I've gotten older and have coached a lot of kids, picked them up, driven them to practices, and brought them food, I've realized something: Coach Hamilton, Coach Wilson, and Coach Elbe taught me at a young age what it means to give back to your players. It's not just about the game. It's really about their journey. It's about them.

Looking back, this was really the first time I experienced a coach going out of their way to make sure I had what I needed. My coaches gave us so much more than instruction on the field. They gave us rides, shoes, meals, sweatshirts—whatever we needed. And that meant a lot to a kid growing up in a single-parent household with three siblings. My younger brother and sister were also heavily involved in sports, playing travel basketball, baseball, and softball, and my older brother loved working on the farm. It wasn't easy for my mom to get us everywhere we needed to go.

But our coaches stepped in. They picked us up, took us to games and practices, and sometimes even brought us food. Looking back, that kind of care shaped who I became. It influenced why I coach and how I coach. Those coaches gave so selflessly, expecting nothing in return.

There are families in our community who stepped in, too—families like the Arnolds, Sharpes, Smiths, and Chillions. Through booster clubs or just simple acts of kindness, they made sure kids like us had meals, access to gear, and support when we needed it.

Our high school basketball coach, Coach Harry Elbe, used to take a group of us to church over in Camp Point. Afterward, we'd head to a little breakfast buffet nearby. I don't remember the sermons, but I do remember the sausage and biscuits. And I remember how those mornings made me feel—valued, seen, cared for.

When I think back on those times, it's clear just how much those coaches influenced the direction of my life. Today, I'm deeply involved with my own family and have been coaching in some capacity for the last thirty-five years, ever since I graduated from college. And I carry their example with me into every season, every team, and every practice.

At the time, we were just kids happy to get a warm meal or a ride to the game. Now, with years of coaching behind me, I see how intentional and generous those coaches were. They gave not only their time, but their hearts. And I will always be deeply appreciative of that.

So, I try to do the same now. I encourage young coaches to understand that this job—this calling—isn't about money. You do it because you love it. You do it because you care. You do it because you want to give kids something that someone once gave so generously to you.

The byproduct is that you get to work with great kids and great families. You get to see them grow, overcome challenges, and become better people. You don't *have* to go to practice—you *get* to go. Sometimes you won't see the fruits of your labor for years, but the investment you make in them will take root in ways you may never fully know. Coaching gives you the chance to impact more lives in one season than most people do in a lifetime.

For me, those early experiences helped me understand that coaching is about so much more than the sport. Kids look up to you. They model your behavior. They emulate you. They want to become you. Especially at the youth level, you're not just a coach —you're a role model, a mentor, and sometimes even a lifeline. You're helping them figure out who they are.

Of course, coaching changes as you progress. At the college level, it becomes more of a business. Winning becomes the focus. But even then, relationships still matter. You still have the opportunity to make a lasting impact on a young person's development.

I've been blessed with the opportunity to coach all over the country—basketball, softball, East Coast, West Coast, you name it. It's been an incredible journey. But more importantly, it's allowed me to give back. Many of the kids I've coached wouldn't have had those experiences unless someone stepped in and said, "Come on. You're going with us."

Work can be rewarding. Family is always rewarding. But your team can become a second family, too. You travel together, share meals in hotel lobbies, spend weekends on the road, and build something special.

That's the kind of reward money can't buy.

That's what I experienced from my own coaches. And that's what I try to give my players now.

Ultimately, make sure your players know you care. There will be pressure—pressure to win, pressure from parents, pressure from your school, or your peers. But pressure is a privilege. It means people are watching, and you matter. It means you're winning not just games, but trust, relationships, and respect.

And if your players know you care, they'll do anything for you. And we don't always know what kids are carrying. Sometimes they need more than a playbook—they need a simple pat on the back, a word of encouragement, a warm meal.

So, to young coaches and families joining these teams: let kids be kids—they want to go to prom, play multiple sports, and enjoy their youth. Don't miss graduations or weddings because of the sports schedule—those are once-in-a-lifetime events you'll never get back. Kids will have conflicts, and that doesn't mean they're not committed.

Let their personalities come through. It's okay if one kid is quiet and shy, and another is outgoing and a little more rambunctious. Ask them for feedback. Learn how to coach those different personalities.

Then it becomes your job, as the coach and leader, to manage and guide that energy in a way that forms a team and allows them to perform at a high level.

As a coach, you have the chance to make a real impact, but you have to actively seek out those opportunities. In fact, many are hidden, waiting to be discovered by someone with the vision to look beyond the surface. And some of these small, hidden opportunities will become the most meaningful experiences of your life. Others may challenge you in ways you never expected.

Finding coaching opportunities is often about being willing to raise your hand. Many youth organizations, rec leagues, and travel teams are looking for committed people. Post on social media. Reach out to local clubs. Talk to high school or middle school coaches, district athletic directors. A lot of sports require multiple coaches—offense, defense, positions—and programs are always looking for help. If you have a connection with college coaches, they are often plugged in and can help you find an entry point, so don't be afraid to ask. If you've got experience or even just interest, you can find a spot.

So, do people really eat chicken wings?

Absolutely. And I'm glad Coach Hamilton handed me that greasy little bag all those years ago. Because what he really handed me that night—what all my coaches at Highland High School gave me—was an example of what it means to care.

That's what coaching is about.

CHAPTER 2
THE DAY I MET THE REAL MICHAEL JACKSON

Monroe City, Missouri, is a tiny little town in Northeast Missouri: population 2,000, no stoplights, one four-way stop, two gas stations, Snack & Pac, and the home of the quarter cake. This is the day that I met a guy named Michael Jackson. The *real* Michael Jackson. He was talented and could probably moonwalk, too!

If you played sports in Northeast or Central Missouri, you knew the Jackson family. They were a legendary group of athletes from Monroe City who played every sport and eventually became well-known across the entire state. Five siblings, all involved in athletics, featured regularly on the front page of the paper and on the nightly local news. So, I had been hearing about this Michael Jackson character for a long time. The only Michael Jackson I'd heard of before him was the one singing "Thriller" on MTV. I'd gotten tired of hearing about this local guy, considering I'd never even met him.

That changed when our Lewis County travel baseball team headed to Monroe City for a doubleheader. Our coach, Bill Robinson, would pile us into a van and drive us to every game. He'd feed us afterward, too, often out of his own pocket. Most of us didn't have much, and Bill made sure we never went hungry. I'll always be grateful to him.

Monroe City had a strong baseball team. And in the top of the first inning, at about 105 degrees that day in June, in runs none other than *the* Michael Jackson out to shortstop—afro barely tucked under his hat. And their pitcher? A guy named Ralph Lemonjell, who looked like he was twenty-five, mustache and all. He threw gas, and we were all nervous.

I was batting cleanup. Our leadoff man, Kevin Lewis, got on, second guy singled with a bloop into right field, third, Roger Alderton, drew a walk. Bases loaded. I stepped in, hoping he'd walk me so I wouldn't have to swing. First pitch whizzed by: ball one. Second pitch: ball two. Third pitch: ball three. On a 3–0 count, I figured I'd better swing, or I'd never touch the ball. And sure enough, Ralph comes out of his stretch and throws a ninety-mile-an-hour fastball. I closed my eyes, swung as hard as I could—and hit a grand slam.

As I rounded second base, this Michael Jackson cat is smiling with his hand out for a high-five. "That's good stuff, Log," he said. No opponent had ever called me that before; only my friends did. And that moment stuck.

Fast forward a couple of months, and we're playing Michael Jackson again. And again. And again. He's the superstar quarterback. He's playing in the basketball conference championship game. He's next to me on the starting blocks at the track meet. Eventually, we became great friends.

We went to college together, played on the same team, lived in the same dorm room, ate every meal together, and danced (well, that's a loose term) at the same parties. We wrestled every day. He says he beat me up; I say I beat him up. He graduates. I graduate. We both move to Columbia.

Attached at the hip, me and MJ—Action Jackson.

Today, we live across the street from each other. We still coach together. We travel with the Missouri Phenom program. We split hotel rooms. We rehash games in lobbies. We hoop in men's leagues. That one summer day turned that competitive spirit against each other into a lifelong friendship.

You never know who you'll meet through athletics. Some of those people become lifelong friends—players, coaches, teammates. And that's the heart of coaching. It goes far beyond the game.

Whether you coach tee-ball or college basketball, it doesn't matter. Coaching is about relationships. Friendships. Mentorship. It's about the kids who play for you and the coaches you stand beside. And if you stick with it long enough, you start to see those relationships come full circle.

I recently had lunch with three Phenom coaches, including MJ. These are coaches, yes—but they're also some of my best friends. We reflected on the network of coaching. You're coaching friends. You're coaching your friends' friends, your kids, your neighbors' kids. And it's through these friendships that you find some that will last a lifetime and become some of your best friends. You're influencing lives. You're shaping families. You're impacting your community.

Experienced coaches: you have a chance to give back in this way. Young coaches don't always know the next step. But you've been there. Share your lessons. Pass on your wisdom. Teach them the Xs and Os—and the human side of coaching, too.

That means managing relationships. Parents. Players. Opponents. College recruiters. Your own staff. Build trust through sweat equity. Show up organized. Stay late. Pick up trash under the bench. Sweep the floor. Be the person who quietly does what's right.

And make it relational, not transactional. We're seeing more and more transactional teams these days, especially with the Transfer Portal in college and the dog-eat-dog world of high-level club sports. But remember, you're building relationships with these players that can last a lifetime. Let players know they matter. Get to know the quiet kid. Teach the vocal leader how to listen. Let kids be themselves. Then coach them into a team.

Relationships extend off the field, too. Go to team dinners. Host coaches' retreats. Seek input from assistants and players alike. Listen actively. Communicate clearly. Overcommunicate, even. Use GroupMe, text chains, email—whatever it takes.

Coaching is a leadership role, and that means modeling character and integrity. Represent your team, your club, your community with pride. Work hard. Laugh often. Be present.

You have a duty and an honor to represent yourself, the team, and the club. Do a great job coaching; the best job coaching that you can. But make it fun. Team dinners are fun. Meeting with the coaches in the lobby to rehash the games from the day, that's fun. We used to give out milkshakes to kids who took a charge in practice. Create your own version of that. Reward effort, not just results. Even when we don't play well or lose, it can still be a learning experience for everyone involved. Sometimes we even learn more through our losses.

Because if you do it right, coaching will give you more than any paycheck ever could.

Michael Jackson gave me a high five that day in Monroe City. And decades later, he still shows up in my life—on the sidelines, in the car, at lunch, in the hotel lobby.

Find your Michael Jackson. They're out there. And they just might change your life.

CHAPTER 3
ON TOP OF THE MOUNTAIN, MY FIRST STATE CHAMPION

After finishing my undergrad at Culver-Stockton College, I headed to Columbia, Missouri, for graduate school to study sports management and exercise physiology. At the time, I figured my competitive sports days were over. I assumed I'd pivot to academics, leave athletics behind, and dive into my studies.

But that fire to compete and coach? It never left. Being in Columbia—home of the University of Missouri and steeped in sports culture—made walking away from athletics even harder than I expected.

Before I ever coached basketball, I ran track. I competed in the 110-meter and 400-meter hurdles in college. In high school, I even placed at state in the 110-meter hurdles. Track had always been a part of my journey, largely because of Coach Hamilton and Coach Wilson—our football coaches at Highland High School. They "strongly encouraged" us to run track, and if you've ever had a high school coach "strongly recommend" something, you know what that means.

When I moved to Columbia, I reconnected with my former college track coach, Coach Leutjen, who had taken a job at Hickman High School. Seeing him again was a blessing. He is a great man—positive, structured in the way he coaches, and deeply passionate about kids and sports.

Then one day in early March, Coach L called me with the question that changed everything: "Would you want to help coach track at Hickman?".

I didn't hesitate. I was living with four other guys in a tiny apartment, surviving on a graduate assistant stipend. The job came with a $1,500 stipend, which felt like a windfall at the time— and more importantly, it gave me a chance to coach.

There was just one catch: I'd be coaching shot put and discus. Two events I had never competed in—and barely understood. Oh, and one of my best athletes? He was the reigning state champion in both events, having already committed to Mizzou on a full-ride scholarship.

Talk about trial by fire. But I loved being around high-level athletes—and people who excel in any area. This was my chance to dip my toes into coaching, an opportunity to spread my wings, work with athletes directly, and make a little money to help pay the rent while in grad school.

I told Coach L I was in, but I needed help. I asked him where I could find drills, how I could become a "mini-expert" in just one week. He gave me the green light to meet with other coaches in the area, soak up as much knowledge as I could, and get ready. There was a coach at the University of Missouri, Coach Edwards, who was an elite throwing coach, renowned across USA Track and Field. Within the industry, he was considered a thought leader.

He connected me with Coach Edwards, and three times a

week, we'd meet and I would soak up everything I could: drills, techniques, troubleshooting, practice structure. We watched film, broke down throws, and he even showed me how to throw shot and discus myself—rain or shine.

He gave me his time, unpaid, out of sheer kindness and love for the sport. I'll always be grateful for that.

That experience taught me one of the most important lessons a young coach can learn: humility is a strength. When you jump into coaching, it's rare that you know everything. In fact, it's rare you know much at all. But you can make yourself better, and that means seeking out advice.

Find a thought leader in that area and ask for help. If that's not possible, go to the head coach and ask them to set up a meeting so you can learn. If you don't have the resources, someone on the staff, at the school, or in the club usually does.

That 1992 season, our defending state champ repeated as champion in both shot put and discus. Our team placed fifth overall, and another one of our throwers placed fifth individually. It was my first year coaching, and I was spoiled with a state champ right out of the gate. I still remember the feeling of watching him stand on the podium, receiving his first-place medal.

That athlete who took fifth still stays in touch. He went on to play football at Evangel and set their school record with a 74-yard punt. Today, he's a well-respected orthopedic surgeon in our area, married with kids. That's the beauty of coaching—you don't just teach athletes. You build lifelong relationships.

Years later, that same willingness to learn reappeared in a new way—when my daughter decided to play softball more competitively.

I didn't know much about softball. I played baseball growing up, but softball is its own game—especially when it comes to pitching and strategy. When Conner said, "Dad, I want to play at a high level. Can you help me get there?" I did what any coach-parent would do: I figured it out.

I may not have known much about softball at the time, but I did know that Mizzou had a nationally ranked softball team. One morning, I drove over to the stadium and knocked on Coach Earlywine's door.

"I'm new to this. I want to help kids get better. Will you help me learn?"

And just like Coach Edwards, he welcomed me in. I watched practices, learned drills, studied game plans. He gave me everything—from strength training to nationally renowned pitching contacts in Doug Gillis and Pete D'Amour. Once again, I leaned on others to grow my coaching skill set.

I still remember when he asked, a few months later, "Want me to teach you how to teach hitting?" He's a nationally recognized hitting coach. I thought he was joking. But for an hour, he broke down video clips and mechanics—from leg drive to wrist action, how to hit a drop ball or a rise ball—you name it.

And it worked. That softball team became one of the best in the country. We played nationally, and several girls went on to play in the Big 12, SEC, and Big Ten. Many others earned spots at mid-major schools—Missouri Valley, Ohio Valley, and Summit League programs. The Missouri Stealth Fastpitch program has produced college athletes across the country, and we're proud of that legacy.

The common thread in all of this? Don't be afraid to ask for help. Surround yourself with experts. Learn from the best. Whether it's your first day or your 30th year, there's always more to absorb.

You're going to learn from a lot of different people and resources, but growth only happens when you're uncomfortable. You might not be great at talking to your team at first—I certainly wasn't. I struggled to stand in front of a group of kids. I stuttered and stammered. I wasn't sure what to say during a timeout. That's okay. That's normal. Discomfort leads to growth.

And as you grow, you become the tilt-o-meter.

That's what I call the intangible role every coach plays. The meter starts at 90 degrees—straight up and down. Your energy tilts the emotional tone. Your attitude tilts the day, the week, and the season—toward focus or chaos, positivity or negativity, joy or frustration. Your job is to tilt it in the right direction.

Always remember that the kids signed up to play for *you*. That's why they're here—whether it's school ball, recreational, semi-competitive, or elite level. Whether they earn a college scholarship or not, they chose *you*.

They believe in you. They believe in your values, your work ethic, and your ability to help them grow. Their parents believe you'll be a positive influence, no matter their child's skill level or goals. They trust that you either have—or will find—the knowledge needed to guide them.

So stay humble. Stay hungry. Ask questions. Soak up everything. Tilt that meter in the right direction. Because when you do? That's when you find yourself back on top of the mountain.

CHAPTER 4
DINNER'S COLD AND THE KIDS ARE SLEEPING

First and foremost, I'm most thankful for my wife, Rachel, and daughters, Conner and Addie. There's no way I could coach effectively without their support and love. That doesn't mean it's been easy.

There have been countless times when I thought I'd be home in time for dinner—but didn't make it. Maybe a player stayed late to work on a skill. Maybe a coach wanted to review film one more time before finalizing a scouting report. Maybe it was something personal with a player, or a pitcher needed to throw a few extra pitches and asked me to catch. These things pile up.

More often than not, coaches get home late. That's life for a coach. Practices in the cold, on wet turf, under flickering gym lights. Rainouts, cancellations, delays. But that also means sacrifice for the family. I've walked in plenty of nights to find dinner in the microwave, the kids already asleep, and my wife exhausted. You wake up, go to your full-time job, change into your coaching gear in the office bathroom, and rush to practice.

Celebrating a birthday dinner with my wife, Rachel, and daughters,
Addie and Conner

That's why I want to talk about keeping your family first. It's not easy, but it's what matters most.

As a coach, one of the loneliest sights is looking into the stands and seeing your spouse sitting by themselves. I've seen Rachel do that more times than I can count. It's not just the coach who sacrifices—our families do too.

Sometimes a spouse sits alone because they can't stomach the disparaging remarks. Maybe someone nearby is bad-mouthing the coach or players. Or maybe there's someone hollering at the referees, and your spouse doesn't want to be a part of it. Either way, it's isolating. And it adds pressure, especially for coaches' kids.

There's a subset of people in this world you'll never be able to make happy, no matter what you do. Even if you're undefeated and top-ranked in the state, there will still be complaints. It's part of the job. And if your own kid is on the team, the scrutiny doubles. They could be Michael Jordan, the fastest 100-meter sprinter, the best shot-put thrower, or the top-ranked volleyball player in the nation, and people will still whisper, "She's only playing because her dad's the coach." You manage practices, games, team communication, schedules, and logistics—and still, sometimes it feels like it's not enough.

It's a no-win situation, and as a coach, you have to be aware. Don't let it steal your joy. Keep showing up with passion and positivity. Because here's the thing: most parents, no matter how well-meaning, have blind spots. We all wear "parent goggles." But at the end of the day, your family is who will be waiting for you when you get home, and there's no better comfort in life than that.

That's why it's crucial to set boundaries. When you leave practice, leave it behind. Go home. Eat dinner. Talk about anything but the game. Ask about school, friends, and weekend plans. Joke about a movie. Laugh with your kids. Let them be kids.

If your daughter strikes out three times and walks five batters in a row—or your other daughter dribbles the ball off her knee and goes one for seven from beyond the arc—so what? Their strikeouts and missed shots won't matter a decade from now. Their self-worth shouldn't hinge on batting averages or shooting percentages.

Early in my coaching career, I tried too hard to avoid the appearance of favoritism. I was so focused on pleasing other parents that it probably came at the expense of my own kid. I gave more time to other kids than to my own. And that wasn't right. My kids deserve the same energy (probably more, to be frank).

Don't make your child the scapegoat just because they're accessible. Don't deflect blame onto them to appease others. They need your support, your protection, and your presence.

You also have to know when to speak up. When the chatter gets too loud, when negativity starts poisoning the team, it's time to lead. Call a parent meeting. Reset expectations. Be clear: you won't allow cattiness or backbiting. Your job is to protect the kids —all of them.

And if you're coaching your own child, be vigilant. Coaches' kids often train harder than anyone. They're around you constantly. They soak up drills and lessons by osmosis. They may be among your best players—and you'll need to be ready for the perception that brings.

But there's nothing more rewarding than coaching your own kid. There's just something unique and awesome about wearing the same logo as your child when they're out there performing. Nothing better than putting your arm around them after a tough game. Carrying their bag. Listening to them vent in the car, not just about sports, but about life. School. Friends. Bullying. Growing up is hard, and being their coach gives you a rare window into their world.

Some of my favorite memories came from coaching my daughters. My youngest daughter played basketball, so I coached a third-grade team called Lady Orange. Most of the girls were teammates in soccer, but wanted to try basketball. We got gym time twice a week—6:30 to 8:00 p.m., thirty minutes across town.

I had a big Ford Expedition for hauling around medical equipment during the day. So I said, "Hey, there's no reason for eight parents to drive thirty minutes one way and thirty minutes back. If you want your daughters to ride with me, I'll take them." We'd meet at one of the players' homes, and eight players would pile in with me.

That team was so memorable. We told ghost stories. We sang songs. We celebrated with milkshakes if someone took a charge in practice. We created memories that still make me smile.

Coaching your kid's team lets you shape the schedule. That flexibility matters. I juggled two elite teams—one for each daughter. I worked full-time in medical sales, but we made it work. We practiced at a facility with a gym and batting cages. With great assistant coaches, I could delegate. At 3:00 p.m., I'd set the schedule for both teams. Softball in the cages, basketball on the court. Drills would start: hitting for softball, three-man weave for basketball.

We called the gym "Key Largo." It wasn't glamorous, but it worked. And we made it fun.

But you have to draw lines. No practices on holidays. No tournaments on Christmas, Easter, or the Fourth of July. Monday and Wednesday nights were for family. Every Friday at 11:30 a.m., I meet Rachel for lunch at Billiard's Burgers. Those habits grounded me.

Coaching is demanding. But you can still have a happy home, coach your heart out, and give your best at work, if you set the boundaries.

And if you're lucky, you'll walk in the door one night and find the food still warm—and the kids still awake.

PART TWO
PRE-SEASON
LAYING THE GROUNDWORK FOR CULTURE AND COMMITMENT

CHAPTER 5
THE WINS, THE LOSSES, AND EVERYTHING IN BETWEEN

Everyone wants to win. But how do we define success beyond the scoreboard? How do we define it at work, at home, with our families, friends, colleagues? Sometimes it's tangible—measured by a scoreboard or sales numbers. Sometimes it's intangible—etched into effort, work ethic, and connections.

Let me tell you about one of the most enjoyable teams I've coached in thirty-five years, all starting in 2024.

Ironically, as I write this chapter, we're preparing to welcome new Nike-sponsored teams into Columbia, Missouri, for their first practice weekend. We always begin on this weekend in March because the Missouri State Championships are happening, and it's the perfect opportunity to watch our players compete in the Final Four while also building chemistry through practices, meals, and team-building events.

Just one year ago, this same week, we brought our 2027 and 2028 teams together for their first practices. We didn't know just how good this group would be. We had a gut feeling. We knew they had talent—maybe more talent than we'd ever seen at those younger levels. They were long, athletic, and tough. But the real question was: could they come together? Could they become a *team*?

With these all-star rosters, everyone is used to being *the* player on their school team. We carry ten elite athletes. High school rules mean four eight-minute quarters—and ten kids can't all play the whole game. Someone's not getting their usual minutes. Someone's not taking 25 shots. So the challenge becomes: how do we build trust, buy-in, and a shared mission?

We started in St. Louis and played okay—not great. We got back in the gym for practice. When I say practice, I mean *practice*. College-level intensity. Three to four sessions in a single weekend. Then we flew to Virginia, practiced Thursday, and played two games Friday, two Saturday, and one Sunday.

That trip to Virginia changed everything. We went 5–0. We left ranked #1 in the Nike EYBL standings out of thirty-two teams. Suddenly, the ceiling got a whole lot higher.

But success didn't come easy. We had a few flat games here and there. We were average in Wichita and Kansas City, then missing players in Arizona. June came, and we took a step back. Players returned to their high school teams, and we supported that. We *want* them to play with their schools. We prided ourselves on working *with* high school coaches—not against them.

In July, we reconvened. We practiced, then traveled to Wichita —where we played poorly. I wasn't there because I had the privilege of walking my daughter Conner down the aisle as she married her husband, Clint. That weekend mattered more than any game.

But what came next was the most rewarding basketball stretch of the entire summer.

During the Division I live viewing period, we played in front of 50 to 60 college coaches each game. We went to Louisville and finished 6–1, beating several top-tier teams. Then, after a brief rest, we headed to Chicago—the final test.

We were the #1 overall seed going in, and we proved it. Undefeated, even dominant, in pool play. A tough overtime win in the first bracket game. A dominant performance in the quarterfinals. Then came the semis—tied with twelve seconds left. We called a timeout, drew up an out-of-bounds play, and our rising 2028 star hit the game-winner.

The championship game was an incredible contest. Tied with seconds remaining, our point guard, Ryenn Gordon, drove to the rim. Floater. Front rim. Back rim. Front again—and in. Buzzer. Game over.

We were the Nike National Champions.

The joy of winning—seeing the smiles on the players' faces, knowing all the hard work they had put in, the practices, the sweat, the tears—it was indescribable. The competition had been fierce, the experience pressure-filled, and the kids wanted to perform well in front of college coaches.

But the joy of winning—and seeing the kids in that moment— is something I'll never forget. The pictures, the championship logo, raising the trophy, seeing the smiles on their faces, and most importantly, the lesson they learned: if you work at a high level, it gives you the chance to win at a high level.

I've felt that joy before. My first coaching job was at Hickman High School, where I coached a state champion in the shot put and discus. Another athlete I coached placed fifth, and we still talk today. He's now an orthopedic surgeon. These relationships? They last a lifetime.

As the JV coach at Rock Bridge during the 1996–97 season, we entered the Final Four 29–0. We lost to a team with an NBA lottery pick and finished third. It hurt—but the journey was incredible.

Coaches, if you and your players commit to the work (and love the process), you'll create something special. You'll see joy and heartbreak, growth and grit. And if you do it right, your team becomes bigger than any one person.

Let me say this clearly: be humble when you win. Arrogance has no place in youth sports. We've seen too much of it—coaches and parents who make it about themselves, not the kids. Don't be that coach. Shake hands. Act with class. Remember, there's no honor in rubbing it in. Just win with grace.

And yes, winning feels *different* as a coach. Better, even. You're the leader. You're developing young people. Whether you're the coach of the speech team, the debate team, the marching band, or the choir, you're responsible for the performance of that team. But the satisfaction of seeing kids develop is paramount.

Now, let's talk about a practical aspect of coaching. After we won that Nike National Championship in Chicago on Monday, my fellow coaches and I woke up and went back to work on Tuesday. Many youth coaches work full-time jobs. Some are in high-stress fields—law enforcement, education, healthcare, or manufacturing.

For me, it's medical devices. I'm in the operating room most days. Coaching is a passion, not a paycheck.

That means making an intentional *transition* from work to practice. You've got to flip the switch. One minute, you're working under pressure. The next, you're leading a group of kids who deserve your full attention and positivity. You may be changing clothes at a rest stop or walking straight from surgery into a gym. But when you arrive, your mindset matters.

So, I just want to offer a vote of confidence: If you want to coach, you *can* do it. You can have a happy home life. You can do a great job being a parent. You can do a great job at work. And you can do a great job coaching. You just have to be intentional about balancing it all.

And remember: when you're at practice, you're all working together. You're one team. Your assistant coaches? You're all on one team. The players? You're all on one team.

Because coaching, like winning, is never about *me*. It's about *we*.

It's not coaches vs. parents. It's not head coach vs. assistants. It's all of us, on the same side, trying to do what's best for kids.

So, what is success? Is it a record? A trophy? Sure, sometimes. But I've coached teams that go .500, that overachieved through pure effort, and winning teams that fell short of their potential. Success is the impact you have on kids. It's what lasts.

As a coach (or even as a parent), you really have to ask yourself: What are you focused on when chasing success? Is it just your win–loss record, or is it the impact you make on kids?

If you want to win at the highest level, it has to be a "we thing," not an "I thing."

And that, more than any championship, is what real success looks like.

CHAPTER 6
THE BALANCING ACT

As we move into the challenge of balancing coaching, family, and life in general, this chapter is about time commitments —how they differ between college, high school, and club levels— and how to find the right starting point.

My true passion has always been basketball. Ever since I picked up a ball in our old barn outside of Steffenville, Missouri (population: 39), I've loved the game and the people it has brought into my life.

Winning a state title in track was incredible, but my heart was always on the hardwood. The question was: how could I get back to basketball while juggling school, work, and bills? I was in grad school, substitute teaching to make ends meet, and didn't have much time or money. I'd earned a basketball scholarship for college and had a mix of loans and academic aid, but life was still a balancing act.

That year, two people changed my trajectory: Gary Filbert, who had recently moved from the University of Missouri athletic department, where he coached with Stormin' Norman Stewart, to launch the statewide Show Me State Games; and Bob Burchard, the fiery, redheaded basketball coach at Columbia College. Both of these men were proven winners and taught me a lot about the juggling act we're discussing in this chapter.

I remembered Coach Burchard from the year before, when I was in college. His team had beaten us in a high-scoring game, and he had a reputation for building championship-level programs. I wanted in.

So I walked into Coach Burchard's office one day and said, "Coach, I want to help. I want to learn. Can I be a volunteer assistant?"

He said yes. "Come tomorrow at four o'clock. We're having open gym."

There was no paycheck. I had rent, car payments, tuition, and not much else. I made money substitute teaching, which in the early '90s paid $75 a day—decent income back then. But the real perk? Two-dollar, all-you-can-eat school lunches. As a broke grad student, that cafeteria tray was gold. Two plates of food and a couple of chocolate milks? Now *that* was living.

At the same time, I started working for the Show Me State Games. The pay wasn't great, but the work was energizing and meaningful. Columbia College added a small stipend—$2,000 a year—to help cover expenses as a full-time assistant. On top of it all, I met and married my lovely wife, Rachel. I was juggling coaching, graduate school, marriage, and substitute teaching.

And I give you: the juggling act.

Young coaches often ask how to balance everything—because the truth is, coaching rarely starts as a high-paying career. It starts as a calling. But that doesn't mean you can ignore the practical stuff—rent, groceries, gas, childcare. You still have to make a living. You have to survive.

At Columbia College and with the Show Me State Games, I was burning the candle at both ends. Weekends were packed with tournaments; evenings were filled with practices, recruiting trips, and scouting visits. Coach Burchard and I spent hours in the car, driving to gyms across Missouri. We practiced six days a week, had film sessions, lifted twice a week, and rarely had downtime. Burchard was a pure winner through and through. It was intense —but unforgettable.

My first team as a paid coach. Full-time assistant in charge of strength and conditioning, recruiting, and scouting. Annual pay: $2000.

What I loved most wasn't just the games or the wins—it was the time with coaches and players, the stories, the laughs, the shared goals. But I was also learning, fast, that time is your most valuable currency as a coach.

That's why you need to be strategic—especially when money is tight, school or work is demanding, and your family is growing.

Eventually, I reached a point where I knew I couldn't keep going at that pace. No matter how important the sporting event, your family comes first. I didn't want to be gone seven nights a week. I didn't want to miss dinner every night or wake up one day and realize my kid had grown up without me. My oldest daughter was just a newborn at the time, and I dreamed of coaching her one day. That wouldn't happen if I were always on the road.

Every coach hits that moment—when you look around and realize something has to give. For me, it was about protecting my family time and stabilizing our finances. It doesn't mean giving up coaching. It just means *finding a version of coaching that works for your life.*

Think of it like a teeter-totter. If your schedule leans too far one way, something else is going to rise—or fall. You have to find the right balance. That means sitting down with your spouse or family and walking through the schedule together. Don't disappear for three nights coaching, scouting, or recruiting, without talking it through. Keep your people in the loop.

Personally, I've always loved being home for dinner. So I started planning practices around that. If I had to travel for a tournament on a Saturday, I'd schedule early practices on Friday so I could be home that evening. Those little changes made a big difference.

These are just a few guiding principles—not only for coaches but also for those striving to be good parents and spouses. We need to be mindful of the effect our absence has on our families, and we must take that into consideration.

Yes, sacrifices come with being a coach. Half the time, you're spending more hours with kids other than with your own. But it's still essential to carve out dedicated time for your family and commit part of your schedule to them.

For young coaches, especially, this is critical advice: start by finding a coaching level that fits your life stage. That way, you can continue coaching and fulfill that inner drive to lead, while still balancing your personal life. Seek opportunities that allow you to grow, learn, and develop as a coach. Surround yourself with organizations and people who are more experienced or qualified. Then, fit those experiences into your schedule in a sustainable way.

You're not going to begin your career coaching in the Big Ten or SEC. That's okay. Pick a level—youth, club, high school—that lets you grow into the profession without burning out or sacrificing your personal life.

At one point, I dreamed of coaching at the highest levels. But I also understood what that would require—and what it might cost me. Instead, I found a path through club coaching that let me control my schedule and stay close to my family.

There will be real questions coaches will need to wrestle with. If you coach a team your kids aren't on, how will you manage missing their games for yours? If you're gone at a tournament on the same weekend your kid has a recital, are you okay with missing their performance? The earlier you think through the tough questions, the better.

Also, surround yourself with people who are smarter than you. Mentors, like the ones I had in Coach Burchard and Gary Filbert, can accelerate your growth and help you learn the ropes more quickly. You'll gain insight into time management, team building, and how to be both a coach and a role model.

Over time, if you become clear on your priorities and continue to grow and surround yourself with the right people, your coaching résumé builds itself. You might start with youth teams and eventually move up to elite travel or even college-level coaching. I've seen it happen countless times. In fact, ten coaches from our club program have recently moved on to the collegiate level—including several who are now Division I head coaches.

The key? Stay committed to your values. Stay committed to your family. Communicate. Take care of those under your roof first, then branch out from there. And find a path that allows you to love what you do without losing the people you love in the process.

So we've come full circle. I walked into Coach Burchard's office as a broke grad student, chasing a dream. I started with no pay, a packed schedule, and a lot of questions. But with the right people around me, and by learning how to balance work, life, and passion, I found a way forward.

And you can too.

CHAPTER 7
MAKING CUTS IS NEVER FUN

As we continue with some of the challenges that coaches face, one of the biggest hurdles is dealing with the uncomfortable moments. These aren't just moments; they can be pivotal in shaping a coach's values and the team's culture. Whether it's breaking tough news to a player who didn't make the team or navigating delicate moments with parents, these conversations will always be part of the job. The goal, always, is to unify—not divide.

I remember the first tryout I ever hosted. I was young and inexperienced entering the world of softball. But my oldest daughter, Conner, had aspirations to play at a high level, and that gave me the drive to figure it out. We promoted the tryout through every possible channel—newspapers, websites, TV, and social media (or at least what existed of it at the time). We needed talented kids and supportive families to build a team from the ground up.

We showed up prepared, and to make sure we were fully

buttoned up, I solicited help from the most organized person I knew and a man who would stand by my side, coaching for years following, Jim Jones. Every player checked in, had their birth certificate, and filled out a detailed information form. We collected everything: positions, schools, throwing hand, batting side, height. We sorted kids by age and position, and I'll never forget one strange coincidence as we sorted players by birthday and age —three of the players were born on Leap Day, including Conner. Another had a birthday the very next day. It was a funny, light-hearted moment that stuck with me. It was also a moment where I started to wonder if this thing could actually work. Maybe that odd coincidence was a good omen.

Coaching my daughter, Conner, at the 18U ASA State Championship tournament. We won the championship game 6-2 with Conner on the mound!

It helps to have a plan for tryouts. Write out the schedule: water breaks, warm-ups, and drills. Know exactly what skills you're evaluating.

At tryouts, we also look for leadership. Who steps up and leads without being asked? Who brings energy? Who shows up with a smile on their face and just makes the whole place feel better? Who encourages others? Who trains on their own, outside of practice and games? The elite players are self-motivated. They put in work when nobody's watching. Many have five-star dreams but one-star habits. We look for the ones who hustle when the gym is empty and no one is watching.

And yes, we evaluate families. Are they supportive? Do they bring drama? Are they switching teams every year or midseason? You need to be thoughtful about that dynamic.

Grades, character, attitude. What do their teachers say? Are they eligible? Are they on time to practice? Are they coachable? Who supports them? These are things that matter to college coaches, and they matter to us.

So, we grouped the players by position, huddled as coaches about looking for hidden talent, and started tryouts. That group turned out to be something special. Many of those players stayed together for years. Some are still close friends. We still keep in touch with their families.

That first tryout taught me something important: even when you feel unsure or uncomfortable, you might still be doing things right. The discomfort means you care. Look for the small pearls in the rough—they'll help guide you through the hard stuff.

Now let's talk about something that's never easy: delivering bad news. One of the toughest parts of coaching is telling a player they didn't make the team. My belief is simple: players come to your tryout for a reason. They believed in your organization. They believed in you as a coach. Their parents are confident that, if selected, you could help their son or daughter grow as an athlete. If a player tries out for your team, they trust you. That alone deserves respect.

Here's how I try to handle it: I always start by calling the players who made the team within 24 to 48 hours. It's important to do this personally, by phone. That's when parents usually ask about the schedule, practice times, and which other players are joining. If a player declines, I move down the list and make another call.

For those who don't make the team, always express gratitude to the players and parents for attending. A text or email can be okay—especially if it's an entry-level team or if you don't know the families personally. But if a player has played for you before and the team has become more competitive to the point where you don't have a spot for them anymore, they deserve a call. It's never fun, but it's the right thing to do.

Elite tryouts come with pressure. Even at the highest level, cutting a player is hard. They might be a superstar, and it's their first time ever hearing "no." When you deliver that news, do it with grace. Explain why. Share what they can work on. Suggest another team if you can. Keep them in the loop. That's how you earn trust.

Often, a kid doesn't make the team because their skill set doesn't match what the team needs. That's not easy to explain to a parent, but it's the truth. Sometimes the second-best eighth grader doesn't make the team because you already have two point guards and need to fill other roles.

This happened to both of my daughters. Conner wanted to pitch, but she wasn't ready for an elite team. She needed reps, coaching, and game experience. She put in the work—lessons, time, focus—and eventually became a top-tier pitcher. But first, she needed to be on a developmental team.

Coaching my daughter, Addie, at the last travel tournament of her basketball career. We came out on top, winning the Basketball on the Bayou tournament in New Orleans!

My youngest, Addie, never played EYBL basketball. She developed on a different path, one that gave her playing time and room to grow. The highest-level team isn't always the right fit.

Even when emotions run high, you've got to stay grounded in your values. You will face pressure to bend your standards. But when you stick to your standards and refuse to lower them, you establish yourself as a leader in your community and in your field. You may lose players because of it, but you'll gain respect. You will face a fork in the road over and over—do you go left and cheat, cut corners, or compromise your integrity to win, or go right and take the high road? Always take the high road.

That includes not speaking negatively about players—especially ones on the opposing team. If you do speak to them, it should only be to say things like, "Hey, that was a nice hit," "Great catch in left field," or "Great hustle diving on the floor." Compliment effort and great plays. Never be the coach who tears kids down. That kind of behavior spreads fast. Coaches talk. Reputations are built on how you handle yourself in those quiet moments when nobody else is watching.

Now, when I'm having a constructive conversation about someone's current skill set—that's different. If I say, "She needs to improve her off-hand," or "If she commits to shooting 100 free throws a week, she can improve her percentage while developing her three-point shot," that's development. That's feedback with the goal of helping a player grow.

If I say, "That player's trash" or "She can't play at this level; they just don't play against anybody, that's why she's good," that's just tearing someone down. When I hear that kind of talk, I usually walk away or stop the conversation altogether. I don't want to be that coach.

Be mindful that after every game, some players face forty-five-minute car rides where only mistakes are pointed out. Use your post-practice huddles to counter that. Tell them directly, "Hey, I'm proud of how you played." Every few weeks, have players form a circle and say one great thing about the person next to them. Build each other up. Praise effort. Praise hustle. Praise growth.

So, keep your language around kids positive. Keep your thoughts positive, too. Encourage players to think positively about themselves. Players become what they repeatedly tell themselves they are.

Is it difficult to make those calls to kids who didn't make the team? Absolutely. It's one of the hardest parts of the job. And if you have a heart, those conversations will hurt.

So be ready for the tough conversations. Young coaches—you are leaders, too. This is where you separate yourself. This is where you become a true leader and an effective coach. When things get tough, don't sweep issues under the rug. Identify problems and address them. Meet with the person. Have the conversation. Dig in. Resolve it. That's one of the most valuable things you can do as a coach, one of the best tools you can carry in your toolbox.

Some players will play multiple sports. That's okay. Some will miss practice for school events. That's okay. We can still create incredible athletes while emphasizing academics and developing young leaders who become some of the most skilled in their field.

We can do all of that—and every part of it matters. And whether a kid plays for our team or someone else's, if they become a better person through the process, we've done our job.

Whether we're at a tryout, a practice, or a game, the most important thing is that we are developing the future leaders of our communities, our states, and our country. If we treat people with respect, support families, and meet their needs—even if it's a player who didn't make the team and ends up joining another club—those players still matter. They are still part of this larger purpose, if we're all doing it for the right reasons.

Keep development as your top priority. Keep the growth of the student-athlete paramount, and you will be successful—regardless of your win–loss record.

CHAPTER 8
THERE'S ENOUGH BREAD FOR EVERYONE TO EAT

This past weekend, I had the honor of hosting all of our top Nike-sponsored teams in Columbia, Missouri. It's always a joy to see the players arrive, and just as exciting to welcome the families who have supported them through long high school seasons. These are the families of kids who have spent months grinding with their school teams and are now returning to the Missouri Phenom program for the summer. There were hugs, laughter, and the kind of excitement that comes when teammates reunite and stories are shared. Some had won state championships. Others reached the Final Four. Many brought home personal accolades. Seeing the joy on their faces filled me with pride.

This year, I was selected to coach the 16U team—a group that brings me genuine excitement. Most of this core team won the national championship last summer, and we've added some talented new players who are already blending well with our culture. Before each practice, we sit down as a group for fifteen minutes. We set expectations. We talk about sacrifice for the betterment of the team. The individual parts alone won't win anything. But if we can unite those parts, the sum becomes something powerful, and the team can accomplish things no one imagined possible. This has always been a core part of my coaching philosophy.

To drive that message home, I walked into our first meeting with a loaf of bread and a box of Ziploc bags. I passed out a slice to every player and had them seal it in a bag, placing it in the side pocket of their backpack, right next to their shoes, jerseys, and gear. We talked about what it symbolizes. In basketball terms, "eating" means playing well, putting up numbers. But on this team, if one player tries to hoard the whole loaf, no one else "eats." If you devour your slice in forty-five seconds, you're out for the summer. But if you share, if you hold onto your slice and play the right way, there will be enough bread in that loaf for everyone to eat all summer long.

This moment always brings out the emerging leaders. You can spot them during warm-ups, during the shootaround, even before we stretch. Some are vocal. Others lead quietly.

One of the biggest challenges is coaching that high-energy, vocal kid. The one who takes over timeouts and organizes the whole team. They're natural leaders, but they can take over if you're not careful. The trick is helping them lead without silencing everyone else. Give them responsibility, but also teach them to listen and step back sometimes.

Then you've got the shy, quiet kid who rarely says a word but might be your most coachable player. With them, you take baby steps. Encourage them to speak up in practice, to lead a drill, to stretch themselves. You can't change who they are, and you shouldn't try. You just help them grow.

And it's a joy to watch both types of kids develop. It's amazing to see a quiet player step up and lead a drill after a little nudge. And it's just as rewarding to see a vocal player learn how to share the spotlight by encouraging them to let others speak and lead during practice. Let the kids be themselves. It's okay if one's loud and one's quiet. It's your job to guide them into becoming a team.

Either way, recognizing these leadership traits early is vital.

———

Remember, almost every one of those players is used to being the star. That's where coaching becomes both an art and a challenge. You have to convince elite players that individual sacrifice leads to team success. That starts with language, tone, and clarity. If you wait too long to address this, you're going to face big problems. Players must hear, early and often, that they won't all be scoring 20 a game or playing every minute. It doesn't mean they're not valued. It means they're part of something bigger.

One coach who models this beautifully is John Calipari. I visited one of his practices at Arkansas earlier this year. He's had rosters full of McDonald's All-Americans, each of them former high school stars. Yet, he routinely brings three or four of them off the bench.

What?! From high school star to coming off the bench?!

At Kentucky, he had Devin Booker—now an NBA superstar and one of the highest-paid players in the league—coming off the bench. His father, Melvin, is a friend of mine from our days at Mizzou. That story sticks with me because it shows that, regardless of what level you're playing at, buying into a team role doesn't limit a player's future. It enhances it.

I've had players who were all-state and averaged 25 points in high school come off the bench on our summer team. That's not easy to accept—because every kid thinks they're going to start and take 18 shots a game, just like they did in high school. But when the team wins, everyone benefits. We had players who scored 6 points per game but ended the summer with nine scholarship offers. Why? Because they bought in. They played team-first basketball. College coaches notice that. They want players who know how to win.

So, to young coaches: Clearly define roles early. Keep pointing to team success. Use real examples like Devin Booker. When players see that the path to greatness includes sacrifice, they'll start to believe you.

College coaches look for players who know how to win, want to win, understand their role, and don't demand 20 shots a game, or to be the shortstop, the striker, or the setter. They want players who accept their role and excel within it. Those are recruitable players.

If you can convince your players that the team comes first, and they're still earning all-conference, all-state, batting .400, or playing shortstop and leading off—then you've done something special. When no one cares who gets the credit, you can accomplish amazing things.

It brings great personal joy when that happens. Players won't always agree with you—and you won't always agree with them. And you know what? That's a beautiful thing. We don't want a team full of clones, where everyone thinks the same. It's okay if a player believes they should be starting, and you think they need to come off the bench. I've had that conversation. And it's okay for them to disagree.

And at the end of the season, when that player opens their Ziploc and finds that stale piece of bread, they'll remember the lesson: if you share the bread, there's always enough for everyone to eat.

PART THREE
GAMETIME
WHERE IT ALL PLAYS OUT—PRESSURE,
PURPOSE, AND PERSISTENCE

CHAPTER 9
YOU ARE, BUT YOU DON'T KNOW YOU ARE

T his is the story of the first team I had the opportunity to lead and coach on my own, with virtually no supervision. I was fresh out of college, a twenty-two-year-old kid who just finished playing at an NAIA school named Culver-Stockton College in Canton, Missouri. It was a small school in the Heart of America Conference, a basketball powerhouse in the early 1990s.

I moved to Columbia, Missouri, to start graduate school for exercise physiology at the University of Missouri, but I wanted to stay close to the game that had already given me so much. Coaching intimidated me a little; the idea of being responsible for a team and its outcomes felt overwhelming. I wasn't sure I was ready to be called a coach, but it had always been something I wanted to do.

Soon after I arrived in Columbia, I started playing pickup basketball in the afternoons at Brewer Gymnasium on campus. The games were feisty, fast, and competitive—often consisting of Mizzou's Big Eight players and elite local high schoolers who slipped in through side doors. These high school kids were local celebrities, often on the news and on the front page of the paper.

One day, a few of those high school kids approached me and asked if I'd coach their AAU team. The roster included some local stars: Rocky Henry (who would later play in the NFL), Kevin Sprouse (an elite high school athlete), and Tom Hart (who now announces on the SEC Network). They had formed their own team—they just needed a coach. They knew I was new in town, a decent player, and hungry to coach. So, I said yes.

Our first practice was at Hickman High School. I was nervous. Nine high schoolers were looking at me, waiting for guidance. So I just dove in.

I showed up with nothing but a few scribbled notes and a head full of drills I remembered from college. We stretched, ran layup lines, and I filled thirty minutes with what I knew. Then we installed some simple offensive and defensive sets. It wasn't polished, but it was a start.

After that first practice, I started doing my homework. I researched drills, studied offensive and defensive strategies, and met with local coaches from Columbia College, Rock Bridge, and Hickman, and with Norm Stewart's assistants at Mizzou. I didn't want to walk into practice number two and look like I didn't know what I was doing.

The second practice rolled around, and I was much more comfortable. Still no assistants—just me and those nine players, all of whom had become familiar faces. That spring and summer, we played in qualifiers in Kansas City, tournaments across Missouri, and AAU Nationals in Omaha.

Keep in mind, AAU basketball and travel sports in 1991 were not what they are today. Today, they are a magnified, multibillion-dollar business where everybody is trying to get a piece of the action and a piece of the money, which comes with much distraction. Back then, kids were just playing for the true love of the game. Back then, these were just nine kids who didn't have a coach and wanted somebody to help them out. Those opportunities will arise for good young coaches if you're on the lookout for them, as we discussed in Chapter One.

I didn't get paid. I paid for hotels out of pocket. And I was dirt poor. But that's how it starts for most coaches.

Opportunities will come your way, but they often require personal sacrifice—money, time, energy. If you're young and in school, you're balancing academics, a job, coaching, and life. If you're older, it might be your family, work, and coaching. But it's possible. You just have to find the balance. You *can* do it.

I coached that team because I loved the game and the kids. Coaching is one of the greatest honors. Even today, I keep in touch with players from that team. I ran into Tom Hart at a Mizzou-Kentucky game recently. I talked to Rocky on the phone last week. Sprousey is a friend for life. It's one of the greatest titles that can be bestowed upon you: *Coach*.

Players remember everything you say and do. They remember your words, your actions, your stories. My youngest daughter, Addie, just reminded me of a New Orleans trip where I jokingly mentioned, and then *actually* played the kids' jersey numbers on the roulette table. It stuck with her. While, yes, I did win and it felt like my lucky day, I knew already that, having the opportunity to coach, it was already my lucky day.

I've coached all over the country, and every place, every team, every player has left a mark. I've attended their weddings, received baby announcements, seen them accepted into med school, or hired as coaches. I've watched players show goats and cows at the State Fair, one even winning the Grand Champion ham! I've been lucky enough to attend countless college signings for kids I coached since elementary school. Those moments are priceless.

So don't forget to tell your players and their families that you appreciate them. They could play for someone else. They chose you. Tell them you're glad they did.

After big practices—sometimes with eighty kids on the court— the ones who come over to say thanks make it all worthwhile. Not every kid will thank you, and that's okay. You do it because you love it, and those high fives and thank-yous become special.

Even when you don't realize it, you're making an impact. Emails, texts, team chats—they all count. Your leadership, your presence, your example of being on time and organized—it all ripples outward. That ripple can be positive or negative. I've seen coaches damage kids without realizing it. And I've seen coaches build a generation through daily acts of consistency and care.

So focus on the person, not just the player. Players will have off days. They'll be upset. Sometimes, the best thing a parent or coach can say after a tough game is: "I love watching you play. I'm really proud of you." No feedback. No breakdown. Just encouragement.

And remember: while everyone wants to bat cleanup and play third base, not everyone gets to be the star. Every team needs role players. Every contribution matters. A tipped ball that leads to a steal can change the game; that backup left fielder backing up third might save a run. See the little things. Recognize them. Celebrate them.

Sometimes, you won't know when you're doing your best coaching. You are leading this group through your leadership, your effort, and your example of being on time, organized, enthusiastic, and technically skilled at your job. You're making an impact that lasts a lifetime—on players, parents, coaches, and the communities you serve.

That first practice at Hickman, I didn't know what I was doing. I wasn't sure I was a real coach. I didn't know what kind of leader I could be. But the truth is—just by showing up, just by stepping out of your comfort zone and trying, just by caring—I was already coaching. I just didn't know it yet.

You are coaching. Even when you don't know you are!

CHAPTER 10

SOMETIMES YOU CAN'T LET THEM PLAY, EVEN IF THEY WANT TO

This chapter starts with the story of my younger brother Troy's basketball team and one of my first experiences dealing with an injury, albeit a minor one. In today's world, injuries play a big role in determining your roster and lineup. Beyond physical setbacks, we also need to keep an eye on players' mental health and stress levels while they're competing and practicing.

Back in 1987, I was a senior at Highland High School in Ewing, Missouri. It was an incredible time and place to go to high school. Ours was a small, tight-knit community, and everyone knew everybody. On game nights, the entire town came out to support us. The crowds were loud and passionate and packed into the gym, which we proudly called The Cougar Palace.

Coach Elbe named it that because he wanted it to be one of the toughest places in Missouri to play. And he succeeded. We prided ourselves on tough defense, hustle plays, and most importantly, winning together as a team. Coach Elbe also used to tell us to make "popcorn plays": highlight-reel moments so exciting they'd make fans jump up and their popcorn would fly all over the bleachers.

That year, Coach Elbe gave us seniors the opportunity to give back by running youth basketball clinics for middle schoolers. On the first Saturday of the league, I got to coach the seventh-grade group. My younger brother Troy, an all-around athlete, was on the team with a few of his buddies. One kid who stood out right away was Scott Stiffy. He was already tall and strong, with great hands and quick feet—just a natural athlete.

We went through drills, ran three-man weave, practiced layups with both hands, worked on drop steps and passing fundamentals. We even squeezed in a little defense, though anyone who knows me knows that wasn't exactly my specialty as a player (I like to shoot!). Still, I made a point to talk about it with the younger kids. I wanted them to understand the full scope of the game.

Toward the end of practice, we were about to scrimmage when I noticed Scott limping. I asked him if he was okay, and he told me his new shoes had caused a giant blister. He pulled off his shoe, and I'll never forget it: the entire ball of his foot was rubbed raw, and the back of his heel was bleeding where the blister had already burst.

Scott wanted to play. He was a competitor. But when he looked at me and said, "Do you want me to play?" I realized what a big moment this was. It would've been easy to say yes. I wanted to win, and he was a key player. But I told him no. "You're hurt. There's no reason to make it worse."

He was disappointed, but he sat out. It was one of the first times I had to say no to a player, even when they wanted to play. And as I grew in my coaching career, I found myself facing that same scenario time and time again.

Years later, I ran into a similar situation—not just with a player I was coaching, but with my oldest daughter. It was at the Colorado Sparkler Tournament over Fourth of July in Denver, an invite-only fastpitch event with every big-name college coach in attendance, Conner tweaked her back just before the trip, and couldn't play. We still went. She sat next to me on a bucket supporting her teammates, and I coached the team.

Could she have played? Maybe. But I wasn't going to risk it. Sometimes, even when a player desperately wants to be in the game, we have to be the adult in the room and say no.

And for one last story, we were playing in a softball tournament in North Chicago. It was hot, 90 degrees. One of our best players, Natalie Fleming, came to me before the game and told me she had a migraine. We had a softball team loaded with Division I players, and thirty to forty coaches lined up to watch us every game that summer. Our superstar slugger, a home run hitter who went on to have an illustrious career at Mizzou in the SEC, told me before the game, "I have a migraine. Do you mind if I sit in the car with the air conditioner on while you warm up? I can't be out here to warm up."

My instinct said, *How are you going to play if you don't warm up?* But I kept that thought to myself and said, "Of course. Stay cool. If you feel better, come back."

Ten minutes before game time, Natalie walked in from the

parking lot. She hadn't warmed up, but she felt ready. I put her in, and she crushed it—two home runs and a highlight reel of defensive plays.

The lesson? Be flexible. Listen to your players. Work with the parents. Be human.

This goes beyond youth sports. Whether you're coaching, teaching, parenting, or managing a team at work, your role is to lead with care. What's best for you in the short term might not be what's best for the group or the individual.

When it comes to injuries, be vigilant. Know what's serious and what's not. Ask questions. Watch for signs. Sometimes it's as simple as asking, "How are you feeling today?"

to show you care enough to ask. Athletic performance on the field will always be secondary to the person's well-being.

On the note of having kids on the team, you always want to treat the players on your team the way you would if they were your own children. Ask yourself: *What would the parent of that kid want from a safety and stability standpoint?* By doing this, you really help foster the child's love for the game.

Conner was little when I first signed her up for peewee hoops at the old Rothwell Gymnasium on the Mizzou campus. (It has an Olympic-sized swimming pool with a lazy river, massive TVs, and a few treadmills sprinkled in now, but back then it was a proper gym.)

The league was run by my good friend, David Johnson (DJ), a Missouri basketball legend who also made a name for himself in

Australia. I figured I'd coach Conner's team. I had the background, and it sounded like fun.

But what I didn't know was that Conner didn't want to play with eight strangers.

At the first game, in her little yellow t-shirt, she asked not to be in the starting lineup. I said, "That's fine. You can come in off the bench." At the youth level, you want to make sure everyone is playing, getting pretty equal minutes, and having fun. If everyone plays and gets quality minutes, they develop more. And if they play, it's more fun. But when it came time to sub her in, she refused. I coached the entire game, and my own daughter didn't play a single minute.

I kept coaching the rest of the season, but Conner never came back to another game. If I had forced her to play, she would've hated basketball. She might have walked away from sports altogether. That experience taught me a powerful lesson: kids need to play because they want to—not because you want them to.

After that season, we made sure to let Conner (and later, Addie) help pick their own teammates. They chose friends, made it fun, and stayed involved. The game became something they looked forward to, not something they dreaded.

When a child's love of the game grows and you don't force them to play, they naturally become more engaged. When parents and coaches force kids to play, the kids often end up burning out early. They lose interest in the sport entirely and can't wait to quit and walk away from it. The goal is to allow them to love and enjoy the game. When they do, they'll want to go practice on their own.

Addie, my youngest, loved basketball with a passion. She

would work out in the mornings with her high school team, shoot on her own mid-day, take a nap (she loves her naps!), and do skill training in the evenings. Two or three workouts a day, not because we pushed her—but because she wanted it.

That's what happens when a kid truly loves the game and that love is nurtured by trust, safety, and joy—not pressure.

Sometimes kids want to play, and they can't. Other times, they don't want to play—and you shouldn't force them. As a coach or parent, your job is to discern the difference and always prioritize the child's long-term well-being.

One resource I always recommend is USA Basketball. Their SafeSport program offers training in injury prevention, safety protocols, and how to handle sensitive situations. Their website also breaks down drills and skills by age, grade level, and development stage. They cover everything, from health and wellness to bullying and social issues.

Another great tool? Player ownership. Let your athletes have a say. Let them help coach during practice. Ask them for feedback. Let catchers call pitches, shortstops position the defense, and point guards set up plays. When they take the lead, they learn more. When they make mistakes, they grow.

So here's the big takeaway: Sometimes, you can't let them play —even when they want to. And sometimes, you shouldn't make them play—even if you want them to. Is this something that needs to be monitored? Is this a broken bone that needs to go to the emergency room or urgent care? Or is this someone who just needs rest? You need to be qualified enough to help, and make those decisions in the best interest of the family and the player. If you lead with care, empathy, and awareness, you'll create an environment where they can thrive.

Always put the player first. Treat every kid like they're your own. Help them build a love for the game, and the rest will follow.

CHAPTER 11
WE NEVER LOSE, WE ONLY LEARN

There's a lot of pain and agony that can come along with athletics—not only for players, but for coaches and families, too. Every game has a winner and a loser, every season has an ending, and sometimes, the sting of a tough loss or final game lingers far beyond the final buzzer. If we don't learn how to process those moments, they can follow us for years. So how do we deal with them? What can we learn from them? And how do we help others through them?

One story I'll never forget: the buzzer going off in my final high school game, and again in my last college game. After the handshake line, I walked into the locker room, and it hit me. That was it. I just played my last game with that group. My teammates. My coaches. My school. That wave of finality is a heartbreak I'll never forget. I remember sitting in the locker room both times, tears in my eyes, struggling to take off my uniform and pack my bag. In high school, one of my best friends, Rob Hill, was by my side.

Whether you're a player or a coach, those moments can be incredibly tough. So I want to offer a few thoughts—some perspective, and a few tips—for navigating them.

FOR PLAYERS

What do you say when you've just played your last game? Most of the time, there are no words. You feel numb. You've given your all—your time, your sweat, your energy—and just like that, it's over.

Here's the biggest piece of advice I can give: focus on the relationships.

When the scoreboard shuts off, what matters most are the bonds you've built—with teammates, coaches, trainers, even team managers. Sports are relational, not transactional. And while the pain of your final game may blur everything in the moment, over time, it's those relationships that will stay with you and carry meaning.

To this day, I have great relationships with nearly all my high school and college teammates. And they've mattered far more than the outcome of any one game.

FOR COACHES

Losing hurts. Especially that final game of the season. Thanking players who gave you everything, knowing it's the last time that group will be together—that stings in a different way. But as a coach, your job is to help your players process it, while also managing your own emotions.

You'll have tough conversations. You'll have to talk to the

player who didn't perform as they had hoped. Maybe it was a sold-out gym, a big playoff game, and they didn't hit their PR or make the big play they dreamed of. It's not always a lack of talent —sometimes, it's just the inability to perform at that certain time under those particular circumstances.

Coaching isn't just about drawing up plays. It's about navigating emotions, setting expectations, and leading people. Sometimes you just don't have the horses to beat a top-tier team. At the high school level, you don't get to draft your roster. And that's okay. Your job is to get the most out of the group you have.

And you'll need to support yourself. I'm fortunate to have a wife and kids who are incredibly understanding. After a tough loss, I know I can get in the car or come home and not have to relive it all. That helps more than I can say.

So coaches, when you lose big games, sometimes you won't be able to sleep at night, and you're going to ache from those losses for a long, long time. A lot of times, though, when you're coaching at the youth level, the kids just want to have fun. They want to play, they want to smile, and they want to have a good time. And when the buzzer goes off and the game's over, you want to make it fun enough that they're not stressed about losing.

No one wants to lose. No one likes to lose. It feels really bad to lose. And it feels a lot better to win. But as a coach, you take losing in stride and remember the bigger picture. It's about the players, it's about the relationships, it's about the development of the team. And then, did you perform at the level expected based on your talent?

One year, I was part of a team that went 30–1 and made the Final Four in the biggest class in Missouri. The next year, we graduated four college-bound players. We went .500. Then we went .500 again the following year. But I still count those seasons as successful. Why? Because we got better. The players developed. We competed. And we stayed together.

Sometimes the best coaching jobs happen in seasons when you don't win many games.

First head coaching job: Sophomore and JV Head Coach, and Varsity Assistant with Rock Bridge High School. Coaching ninety games a year with an annual salary of $2050.

In youth sports, especially, winning isn't everything. Development is. From a young age, players mirror your behavior as the coach. If you're composed and respectful, your players will reflect that. If you're throwing clipboards and berating refs, they'll reflect that, too. That's not the example we want to set. When kids have fun, they stick with it. When they stick with it, they improve.

There are also teams that win, but their kids are miserable. I've seen kids who couldn't wait for the season to end, despite winning games. That happens when coaches push too hard or care more about their record than the kids in front of them. We don't want that. We want a win–win: kids having fun, developing, and learning. That's what makes it worthwhile.

Coaches should also be thinking about the growth of their assistant coaches. Are you helping them get better? Are they leading drills, calling plays, running timeouts? Or are they just standing there? Part of your role is growing leaders—on the court, and on your staff.

Same with your players. Did they improve their strengths and build up their weaknesses? Did the team get better from Week 1 to Week 10? That's what matters.

And at the end of the year, how did we play? Did the team improve? Were we better each week? Did we have a plan each week to compete and develop?

Depending on the age group, you've got to coach them individually. A sixth-grade rec team doesn't need the same approach as a high-level 17U travel team. Know your group. Know your voice. And know that sometimes, it's better not to say what you're thinking.

Trust me, I've been married for thirty years and have two kids, so I know the lesson is true: you can't always say what you're thinking.

Most importantly, we want to empower our players. That means letting them make some decisions. That means living with their mistakes. That means letting them learn. Because that's what this is all about.

And understand, as a coach, you can't make every single decision. Whether you're a coach, a player, a business leader, a community leader, a business owner, or a spouse, you're not physically going to be able to make every decision within your ecosystem.

We want the decision-making process to be a mile wide and an inch deep, so that every single player, every single coach, and even our managers, trainers, and administrators feel like they're part of the decisions. That's a true team.

Because when we lose the right way, we don't really lose.

We learn.

CHAPTER 12
DID THAT REALLY JUST HAPPEN? (DON'T BE THAT PARENT)

id that really just happen? It's a question coaches find
themselves asking far too often. Whether it's at the gym,
the softball field, or the soccer pitch, we've all witnessed moments
that make us shake our heads in disbelief. Coaching in group
settings, especially with a wide range of skill levels and multiple
assistant coaches, means these moments aren't rare—they're
almost routine.

Some of the scenarios I've seen could fill an entire book. But
for now, I want to focus on the essence of what it means to
manage these wild situations, especially when it comes to dealing
with parents.

New coaches, listen closely: this will be one of your biggest
challenges.

Experienced coaches: you know this isn't going away anytime
soon.

And if you haven't faced it yet, trust me—you will. My hope is
that this chapter helps you prepare for the inevitable.

We've all seen it: videos flooding social media of coaches arguing with officials, fans storming courts, physical altercations, and parents clashing with coaches. Shockingly, there have even been incidents involving weapons at youth sporting events. Something meant to be fun and recreational turns into a dangerous scene—it's hard to believe, but it's real.

To highlight how serious this is, and hopefully help prevent some of it, I want to share a few stories and insights that might even make you chuckle—if only because sometimes humor is the best way to cope.

Before each season, we send parents a comprehensive email outlining our best practices, policies, and expectations. But more importantly, we hold a live, face-to-face meeting to review those expectations with parents and players. This happens whether I'm coaching a youth recreational team, an elite travel squad, or a school team. That face-to-face connection is critical.

Define your non-negotiables. What behaviors warrant dismissal or consequences? What are your team policies? Know them before that first meeting. I know mine, and I'm more lenient in some areas than other coaches because I prioritize players, families, and personal dynamics.

At the college level, parental involvement is naturally less, since players live away from home. But at the youth level, you'll be dealing directly and regularly with parents. You must be ready for the challenges that come with that.

A hilarious (and revealing) story comes to mind. After a detailed parent meeting and a follow-up email, the season started. At the first tournament, one of our stronger teams struggled in the second half of the *first* game. Coaches made some lineup changes, trying to find a rhythm. But within ten seconds of the game ending, a parent who attended the meeting sprinted up to the coach, demanding to discuss their child's playing time. After just *one* game. The look on our coaching staff's faces was priceless. If only we could've inserted a laughing emoji right there.

I asked the parent if they remembered the meeting. They did. Did they read the email? Apparently not. *Reminder to players: make sure your parents read the emails!*

Parents and kids forget: "parent amnesia" is real. You'll have to explain things multiple times, and that's okay. Mistakes happen, and things get lost in translation.

Once, I asked a player to step into the lane and call a timeout before the referee handed the ball to the free-throw shooter. She forgot. The referee handed the ball to the shooter, and then she called a timeout. Because she stepped in too late, we got a lane violation. We still got the timeout—but it was a learning moment. Mistakes are opportunities to grow and learn.

You'll repeat yourself a lot. Reinforce what's appropriate, when it's okay to contact you, and what's off-limits (for me, discussing playing time during a tournament). Your clear communication can help prevent the volatile, sometimes violent behavior we occasionally see.

Even with proactive, clear communication, parent-related issues will arise. Parents love their kids fiercely and sometimes feel the rules don't apply to them. The pressure to see their child succeed can cloud their judgment, causing them to ignore everything they've been told.

Some parents and players will always believe they're immune to rules and procedures. They expect to come and go as they please, to be catered to, and to be treated differently. These are the tough cases, and they're often tough from day one.

Recognize that parents view their kids through those "parent goggles" we talked about. A kid can strike out four times or have six turnovers, but the parent might insist their child had a great game. It's rarely the kid's fault when the team struggles—it's always someone else's. That perspective can make your job harder.

As the coach, you're often coaching the parents, too. You also have to remind parents: don't be the reason officials stop a game and make you leave. It's embarrassing for everyone—the kid, the team, the program. Parents screaming at referees isn't just disruptive; it's damaging. As a coach, you need to handle those conversations privately, away from the crowd, because it's embarrassing to the player and undermines the team.

Many parents carry more pressure than their kids do. Some push their kids into sports they don't love, living vicariously through them. It's important to notice that dynamic, because it affects the player, the team, and the family. Parents coaching from the sidelines only adds to the confusion. Kids can't listen to two conflicting voices—the coach on the field and the parent in the stands. That's why it's often better to address these issues directly with parents, not kids. Everyone needs to be clear about who's in charge. Drama, whether on the field or at practice, is toxic. No amount of money or success is worth bad vibes.

On road trips, be mindful of what I call "hotel lobby drama"—parents gathering to complain or stir negativity. The lobby is for eating pizza, not for gripe sessions. It's best to nip it in the bud before it even starts.

Social media is another area where parents and players need coaching. What gets posted online can affect recruiting and team chemistry. Cryptic or negative posts are easily interpreted by college coaches and administrators—and can have real consequences. Talk early and often with your team and parents about the impact of social media.

As for setting boundaries with parents, trust your gut. Sometimes, you may have to cut a kid loose if the parent's behavior harms the team. It's a worst-case scenario, especially when the kid is a good kid. Even then, volunteer to help them find another team. I always encourage parents to find the best spot for their kid —and sometimes, that spot is somewhere else.

Always act with class. Don't let parental behavior damage your program's reputation. If yelling and confrontation happen, it's your responsibility to address it promptly and clearly. Set expectations early: playing time discussions should happen after games or tournaments, not during. We've had instances where parents walked up behind the bench during a basketball game their kid was playing in to confront a head or assistant coach about playing time. Yes, that happened during a game—with college coaches watching and potential scholarships on the line. That is never acceptable.

There are levels to this, as my friend Terry Nooner says. Younger leagues often have the wildest behavior, with parents yelling at referees over minor calls. Your job is to lead, mitigate, and contain that. If you do it well, you'll hear fewer people saying, "Did that really just happen?"

Lastly, understand the four distinct roles at every game: player, coach, official, and parent. When I walk into a venue as the coach, I'm not the referee, I'm not the player, and I'm not the spectator.

When the parent is a spectator, they're not the coach, they're not the official, and they're not the player.

When a player is playing, they're not the coach, and they're not the official.

Know your role, and don't cross over. Hybrid roles rarely end well. As a coach, our job is to focus on what's best for the athlete and team, set clear policies, and remind everyone of why we're there: for the athlete and their development.

In the end, managing parent behavior is as important as coaching the team. When you do it well, you create an environment where kids can thrive, and the only question left is: "Did that really just happen?" Because hopefully the answer will be a resounding, "No."

CHAPTER 13
NAVIGATING YOUR FIRST HEAD COACHING JOB

T he process and uncertainty of leading a team, no matter the level, can be nerve-racking. The thought that you are ultimately responsible for your players while they're on the field or court is enough to keep you up at night when you first step into coaching. I want to share the story of the first team I ever led and some of the feelings I experienced. And I want to reassure new coaches: feeling nervous when you're starting out is completely normal.

I still remember the first practice I was in charge of. It was my third year coaching at Columbia College, an NAIA powerhouse in Columbia, Missouri, led by the legendary Bob Burchard. He had transformed the program into a winner from the first day he walked on campus. That week, he had to attend a national coaches' meeting, and he asked me to run practices in his absence.

We practiced twice—Thursday afternoon and again Friday morning. I remember walking into the gym, players shooting around, my clipboard in hand, nerves buzzing through me. Our staff included a graduate assistant, usually a part-time coach finishing school in town. For 48 hours, we were in charge—and just praying nothing major would go wrong. I did not want to screw this up.

I huddled the team up and gave a quick overview. My voice trembled—it was scratchy because I was so nervous. There I was, a twenty-three-year-old man leading a group of eighteen to twenty-three-year-olds, some of whom I'd played against in college. Now I was their coach. But you know what? Practice went great. And the next morning? Even better.

Players respond differently to assistants than to head coaches, but I'll never forget how much fun those two days were. It gave me a taste of what head coaching could be.

Later, I moved to a local high school because of the time demands of college coaching. College ball is a 24/7 job. At Rock Bridge High School, I became the JV head coach and varsity assistant—my first official head coaching position.

Even with years of assistant experience, being the one in charge was nerve-racking. Everyone, fans, referees, players, and parents, was watching. Everyone had opinions. That pressure was real.

The Rock Bridge boys had a very strong varsity team that year. As the JV coach, you're essentially responsible for developing the next wave of varsity players. I felt like it was a great move for me where I could try, potentially make mistakes, and learn in a low-risk environment.

You're going to feel anxious. Your throat might get tight the first time you speak to the team. That's normal. But remember, being a head coach is an honor that administrators or directors have entrusted to you because they believe in your ability to lead and develop players.

From your first practice to your first game—when you're filling out the scorebook, setting your starting lineup, and facing tough decisions—you'll feel the weight of that pressure. Making cuts or telling a player they won't start is never easy.

Then comes game time. You've written your game plan on the whiteboard. You huddle your team. In coaching, you learn public speaking skills *real* quick. You emphasize a couple of key points, the buzzer sounds, and you're off. Then it's halftime. You've got two or three minutes to communicate, highlighting a couple of things we did well that half and a few minor adjustments that need to be made. And afterward? Win or lose, you gather your team and deliver a message, noting a few things to work on in practice, but ultimately ending on a positive note.

I *always* want to leave the huddle, timeout, postgame talk, or post-practice meeting with something positive—something good that players can walk away with, feeling great about themselves.

Even when things don't go right, they probably did eight things well for every two things they struggled with. Focus on that 80 percent. I once heard a pastor say, "You'll love 80 percent of what your spouse does. The other 20 percent will drive you nuts. But don't let the 20 percent outweigh the 80 percent."

Same with your team. You want to win. You want to be great. But we have to make sure we're not overly focused on flaws. We need to lean into the good—the strengths, the progress, and all the positive momentum.

Don't get stuck on what went wrong. Lead with what's going right.

No matter the level, kids need encouragement. They need joy. Whether it's preseason, skill development, summer league, or tournament time—know what phase you're in and what players need most.

If you're coaching recreational sports, the goal is largely development and fun. As you move up the pyramid to higher competitive levels, positivity remains essential, but players can also be pushed more during games, practices, and tournaments.

Also, know the context: Are we talking about a game, a workout, a skill development session, a practice? Know whether it's preseason, offseason, or in-season. Understand the difference between teaching during games versus teaching during practices.

And watch them closely. Monitor fatigue. Prevent injuries. Protect their mental health. Players perform best when they're supported, not worn down by constant criticism.

As a new coach, you'll probably ask yourself, *Will the players respect me? Will the parents?* Do you have to be liked to be successful? Heck no. What matters more is respect. You don't have to be everyone's favorite—but if you bring passion, awareness, consistent energy, and a solid plan every day, respect will follow.

Is it always about winning? No. Winning matters, but it's not the top priority. It's simply the byproduct of doing things the right way. We want to win and compete—but we also want to teach life lessons. If we allow tardiness and lack of commitment without consequences, we're not teaching anything meaningful. No policies, no consequences = no long-term respect.

I'll never forget my first parent interaction postgame as head coach. My JV team lost by two: 44–42. We ran a last-second play, and the shot rimmed out. A parent waited outside the locker room. My heart sank: *Is this about playing time?* It was.

We had a respectful conversation. After that, I created a 48-hour rule: no playing time conversations until two days after a game. And when asked why a child isn't playing, I ask, "Do you want the truth—or what you want to hear?" Usually, they pause. But if they want the truth, I'll give it, kindly and constructively. Then we make a plan for improvement.

Do players have 100 percent access to me? Yes. Parents? Not always—especially not immediately postgame.

Coaches and leaders: coach for the right reasons. It's not about you. Your identity is not your win–loss record. It's about player development, growth, and love.

That adrenaline rush? It's not for you—it's for the players. They're the ones performing. You're still coaching with energy, but you're the guide.

You will make mistakes. I did. Early on, I made it too much about me. I focused too much on winning. But I learned. I evolved. And I'm proud of that.

Within 90 days, I realized: this is about the kids. Everything I've done since then has been designed to put players first.

That's how I sleep at night, knowing I'm doing what's best for them. That's what coaching is all about.

PART FOUR
POST-SEASON
THE LEGACY WE LEAVE AND THE LOVE THAT LASTS

CHAPTER 14
WHY WE COACH

Why would anyone want to coach? Sometimes you wake up and think, *Why am I even doing this?* But if you understand your purpose—why you coach, why you show up—getting out of bed, putting on your coaching gear, and stepping back onto the court or field becomes a little easier.

This chapter is for coaches and players, but I'll include a few pointers for parents as well. I want to take just a minute to talk about why I got into coaching, and why I'm still here today doing what I love.

For me, it goes back to my mom. She was my biggest advocate and a constant example of selflessness. Growing up, she would remind us of the scripture: *"So the last will be first, and the first last."* (Matthew 20:16, ESV) Her version? *Always be the first person to get in the back of the line and put others in front of you.*

She lived it out. I watched her take money out of her own pocket to make sure kids at our school could eat—keeping in mind, we didn't have much to spare. She would've given the shirt off her back. I am who I am today because I watched her battle through the adversity that comes with being a single mother, and because of a family (aunts, uncles, and grandparents included) that was always the first to reach out a hand to help others.

Where you're from shapes you. I grew up on a small farm near a town of thirty-nine people. In rural communities, you learn that people matter, and those people show up for each other. If it snowed, a neighbor cleared your road. If your car broke down, they gave you a ride. They were never paid a dime, but everyone pitched in.

That mindset stuck with me. Coaching is about serving others. And you'll need that mindset—because coaching will test you. People will doubt you. Talk about you. Criticize you. But if you keep showing up with passion and purpose, you've already won.

Along the way, you'll meet incredible people. Sports and athletics have been among the greatest blessings in my life. I still coach alongside childhood friends. I played under phenomenal coaches with teammates who are still some of my best friends today, even as far back as LaBelle Elementary with the Cougar Cubs. The coach (and the families) are often the glue. As a coach, you're the lucky one—the conduit who helps players build friendships that last a lifetime.

I grew up in a relatively poor household, raised by my single mother. Five people. One bathroom. But we had what mattered, each other. And as a coach, one day you'll look back with pride—not at your bank account, but at the lives you impacted. You'll look back and realize it was never about the money. It was always about the people.

That is why we coach. It's never about us—it's always about the kids.

My high school basketball coach, Harry Elbe, showed us that. He'd sit in his office with us after lunch, telling stories about his legendary teams and investing in our lives. Before we left for fifth period, he'd say, "Hey guys, remember, winners never quit and quitters never win." Between him, Coach Wilson, and Coach Hamilton, they would literally do anything to support their players, all while teaching life lessons along the way, never expecting anything in return. That's coaching.

Many of his players—and players today—didn't have consistent role models. Coaches help fill that gap. We're here to love our players and love the game. If we don't genuinely love it, coaching becomes work, and work becomes a burden.

I've been lucky. In coaching and in my career outside sports, I've never felt like I "had to go to work." Whether in the operating room or on the court, I've done what I love to do.

Another word for role model: *mentor*. I coached with Jim Scanlon at Rock Bridge High School. He's led the same program for fifty years. Five decades! In an era where coaches often leave after a few seasons due to pressure from parents or administration, he's still leading the green and gold. That kind of consistency shapes generations.

I got my head coaching start alongside Scanlon, even coaching his kids at one point. Much of what I've learned has come from coaching with mentors like him—and you can't replace their knowledge or experience.

Just last week, I watched the Final Four at Mizzou Arena—

surrounded by coaches at all stages of their journeys. Some were just starting. Others had decades under their belts. That's the beauty of coaching: it's a lifelong calling.

Week after week. Month after month. Summer after summer.

And through it all, we must keep it about the players. It's their journey, their game, their fun, their growth—not the parents', not ours.

We create the environment. We set the tone. We have the privilege—and the responsibility—to keep it centered on the kids.

And if we want kids to grow, we've got to let them play. They can't sit on the bench 95 percent of the time and still develop. Failure is a necessary part of growth. Losing, struggling, being outperformed—those are opportunities to improve. And when those moments happen, it's our job to empower them, to offer the tools and support they need to get better.

I once saw a commercial where a coach was giving a postgame speech, and a frog hopped by. The kids chased it. And honestly? That's real. Sometimes, they'd rather chase a frog than listen to your speech—and that's okay. Let them smile. Let them play. Let them chase the frog.

You're shaping kids beyond the game. After every game, we clean up the bench area, whether it's ours or not. Early on, I had players who resisted that. "I don't pick up trash," they said. But we talked about it. They did it. And later, one of those same players reminded her teammates to clean up. A college coach once texted me, saying they'd seen her cleaning up after a high school game. She became a two-time McDonald's All-American.

That's coaching. That's growth.

When I got my first JV head coaching job, I was too intense—too negative. I came from coaching college men and didn't understand the needs of high school kids. I focused too much on systems and not enough on relationships. I had to evolve.

You have to know your market. Are you coaching girls? Boys? Youth? High school? College? Elite club teams? You can't coach everyone the same way. If you're working with 8U girls, your tone and style should differ from coaching 18U boys in AAU.

Know your players. Adjust your style. And don't be afraid to change. If your team isn't responding, try a new tone. Ask for feedback. Let them choose the practice playlist. Use humor. Build connection.

Because in the end, that's why we coach: love of the game, love of the kids, and the chance to give back.

Greatness requires adaptability. It requires empathy. It requires purpose. And if you lead with those, you'll never work a day in your life—you'll just keep showing up to do what you love.

CHAPTER 15
MONEY, MONEY, MONEY

Now, because it's in the title of the book, let's talk about money.

"Money is the root of all evil," they say. Around here, we say: "It ain't about the money."

We talk about money all the time—when we're job hunting, buying a car, purchasing a home, or planning a vacation. And in youth sports, it's no different.

"What's it going to cost for my kid to play?"

"How much are the hotels?"

"I have to book airfare."

"How much is gas?"

It's money, money, money, money, money.

But for you, coach, money will be reason number 120 for doing this. And if you're coaching for the right reasons, it will never be about the money.

Yes, some coaches make millions at the pro or collegiate level. But most of us are coaching at the grassroots level—entry-level college, high school, club, AAU, youth leagues. And at that level, it's not about money. You'll know that the moment you take your first coaching job. If you're getting paid anything, it's a bonus.

If you're coaching for a living, of course, you need to get paid. Coaches have bills. But when you find the right fit—the right job, the right team, the right culture—money becomes secondary.

I've interviewed for just a handful of jobs in my life, and I've never led with pay. I always start with this: *Is this the right fit? Is this the right place for me, and am I the right coach for them?*

I've always stressed this to every company I've interviewed with, and to every candidate I've interviewed to hire: You can grow into the money. But you can't grow into a bad fit.

No paycheck makes up for toxic parents, a disconnected team, or an unsupportive administration. But the right fit? That's everything. When you love the people you coach and the people you coach with, at that point, the paycheck doesn't matter.

And listen: your first coaching job probably won't be your dream job. Maybe you want to coach a college team one day, but you're starting out coaching U12 girls' rec softball. That's okay.

Dip your toe in. Jump in. Go all in.

If you work hard, if you stay committed to learning and growing, you'll get where you want to go. And when your foundation is love for the game and love for the kids, your path will unfold.

I say this all the time: *coaches often impact more people in a week or month than most people do in a lifetime."* The impact you can make over a long, sustained coaching career is incredible. You'll have the chance to do meaningful things—to change lives—and the number of people you'll reach by working with kids will be far greater than you can imagine. And for me, that's worth more than any dollar amount they can pay.

Growing up on a farm, I learned daily about hard work. About showing up on time. About taking care of people. About following through. About doing what you say you'll do.

Those lessons from the farm shaped the coach I became, and still strive to be.

Dinner might be cold when you get home. The kids might already be asleep. But that's part of the package, the cost. And if you're in it for the right reasons, it's worth it.

People ask me what's kept me coaching for thirty-five years. My answer is simple: It's all about the kids. And it ain't about the money.

Surround yourself with players, coaches, and families who love the game. Be the first to practice and the last to leave. And remember: you don't get to have a bad day. You set the tone. Bring the energy and the passion—every single time.

Comparison is the thief of joy. Don't worry about who's getting paid more, who has a fancier title, or who's coaching the top team. It's not worth your mental energy, stress, or time.

Instead, focus on your team. Be the best coach you can be for the kids you have today.

Go home and be the best spouse, the best parent, the best friend you can be. Because this career is sustainable when you lead with gratitude, with respect, and with love.

You know by this point that coaching is not transactional. It's relational.

It's not about a handshake and moving on. It's about shaking hands, looking your players and parents in the eye, and committing to doing your best, delivering on what you promised—every day.

That's when the magic happens.

That's when players stay in touch, long after they graduate. That's when you get wedding invites, baby announcements, and texts from kids you coached fifteen years ago. That's when you get a call because a former player's spouse just matched at Mizzou Med School and needs a rental home. Those are the calls that will mean more than any win–loss record.

That's the win.

That's why we coach.

So, how do we make this career sustainable?

You've got to plan. You've got to communicate. You've got to prioritize your people and find time to take care of yourself as well.

You've got to have the support of your spouse and your family; they play a vital role in your coaching journey. I couldn't do this without Rachel. I was fortunate that my kids played for me. But now, even when they don't, I still need my family behind me.

Coaching requires sacrifice of many kinds. But with the right support system and a heart centered on servant leadership, you'll find your balance. You'll stay healthy—physically and mentally. You'll find joy.

CHAPTER 16
FOR THE LOVE OF THE GAME

We've talked a lot about love—love for the sport and the people you're surrounded by. Let's drive home the point of why you get into coaching, why you stay in it, and why you wake up every morning and do what you do. You have to love it to stay in it for the long haul.

It's not just a job you bounce in and out of. A coach isn't someone who's here one day and gone the next. Once coaching gets in your blood, it stays there. For many of us, it's a lifelong commitment.

Coaches, you know by now it's going to take a lot of time. It's going to create a lot of stress. Sometimes, you're going to deal with verbal abuse. In some cases, you've even seen physical abuse directed at coaches. There may be tension at home, too, because you're spending so much time with other people's kids while your own family is waiting.

But you can manage it with clear communication, with boundaries, and with purpose. And the key to making it through all the tough moments? Love. That's the foundation.

If you've got a kind, giving heart and you're in it for the right reasons, you'll be coaching for the love of the game. I often see teams that are winning, but the kids are losing. I've seen it season after season. Programs racking up wins, trophies, banners—and yet, the players are disengaged, defeated, and done. They can't wait for the season to end.

What kind of culture are we creating when that happens?

I spend time on the AAU circuit each summer, watching elite athletes and programs from across the country. The level of play is phenomenal. The coaching can be, too. Many of the coaches I meet go on to big-time high school or college coaching jobs.

But even in those arenas, I've seen the warning signs: players emotionally drained, disconnected, and burned out. Teams are winning. Coaches are posting about it on social media by Monday morning. But the players? They're not smiling. They're not thriving.

When the scoreboard says *win*, but the players are losing, we've missed the mark. As a coach, you have the power and the *responsibility* to change that. To create something better. To build a culture that puts people first.

You can feel it when it's wrong. You can sense it when the culture is off. And when you see it, name it. Shift it.

You won't make everyone happy. That's okay. Don't try to. If you do, you'll only end up frustrated. But know this—you'll still receive enjoyment and positive feedback from the vast majority of those you coach, if you just give your best effort. Bring passion. Do the best job you can.

There will always be a small subset of people who are never satisfied, even if you're a volunteer coach spending your own money on hotels and travel. Some will gripe, complain, and be grumpy in the hotel lobby late at night. Let it go and focus on what you can control: your passion, your presence, your preparation.

The best coaches I know bring energy from sunup to sundown. They're there when others are struggling. They're the call that comes when life gets hard. They're still coaching, long after the last game.

Even after retirement, I've seen coaches stay involved (mentoring, consulting, supporting programs) because the love of sport never leaves. I hope this book has helped aspiring and seasoned coaches understand that you can live a full life, serve others, and still lead purposefully. You can coach and have a family. You can pursue excellence without sacrificing your values. With intention and heart, you can make it all work.

Because coaching is a calling.

Coaching can be your mission trip.

Some people travel across the world to serve others. That's beautiful and meaningful. But for me, every July becomes my mission trip—coaching in Louisville, then heading to Chicago for Nike Nationals. That's where I pour in, give back, and find deep personal meaning.

You can do the same. Whether it's spring travel, summer ball, or fall league, your coaching journey can become your mission trip. When you lead with heart and purpose, your impact will last far beyond the final score.

Let me remind you of something important: **you're doing work that changes lives**.

It doesn't just impact the kids you coach; it ripples out to their parents, their peers, your fellow coaches, and the communities you serve. But the most surprising transformation? The one that happens in *you*.

Coaching will stretch you. It will challenge your patience, your time, and your self-confidence. It will bring moments of joy, heartbreak, and growth you never saw coming. But if you lead with love, and if you keep the kids at the center, coaching will make you a better person—a better parent, spouse, teammate, and friend.

If you're in it for the right reasons, fulfillment will follow. Not the kind that shows up on the scoreboard, but the kind that fills your heart and fuels your purpose. You'll find yourself doing something you love, day after day, year after year.

When the season ends, the relationship doesn't. That bond lasts long after the final buzzer, final out, or final goal.

Let's also look out for our fellow coaches. Relationships extend not only to players and families but also to colleagues and even competitors. Be a leader. There will be times when other coaches need your support, too.

Because in the end, it's not about money. It's not about wins and losses. It's about *people*.

We coach for the love of the game.

We coach because it matters.

We coach because we care.

We coach because it changes lives.

And if you lead with that kind of heart—one grounded in service, humility, and passion—then coaching will bless your life in ways you never imagined.

Keep showing up.

Keep giving back.

Keep coaching for the love of the game.

THANK YOU

To everyone who picked up this book: thank you. When I started writing, I wasn't sure if anyone would care about what I had to say. But the fact that you're still here means the world to me.

My hope for you is simple: **go make the world a better place.**

If you're new to coaching, find that first opportunity. If you're already coaching, stay excited about the work you're doing. The opportunity you've been waiting for? It's here. Now is the time to seize it, step into leadership, and make a difference.

Lead with love. Coach with purpose. And never forget:

It ain't about the money.

Best of luck to you all.

—Greg

THANK YOU FOR READING MY BOOK!

I'd love to connect and stay in touch!
Scan the QR Code:

I appreciate your interest in my book and value your feedback, as it helps me improve future versions. I would appreciate it if you could leave your invaluable review on Amazon.com with your feedback.
Thank you!